Contents

Words appearing in the text in bold, **like this**, are explained in the Glossary.

 Find out more about how things are made at www.heinemannexplore.co.uk

What is in chocolate?

Most people enjoy eating chocolate. Chocolate contains some things that are good for your body, but eating too much chocolate can be unhealthy.

How Is Chocolate Made?

Angela Royston

Heinemann
LIBRARY

Young Explorer

www.heinemann.co.uk/library
Visit our website to find out more information about Heinemann Library books.

To order:
 Phone 44 (0) 1865 888066
Send a fax to 44 (0) 1865 314091
Visit the Heinemann Bookshop at www.heinemann.co.uk/library to browse our catalogue and order online.

First published in Great Britain by Heinemann Library, Halley Court, Jordan Hill, Oxford OX2 8EJ, part of Harcourt Education. Heinemann is a registered trademark of Harcourt Education Ltd.

Editorial: Lucy Thunder and Louise Galpine
Design: Jo Hinton-Malivoire and AMR
Illustration: Art Construction
Picture Research: Melissa Allison and Debra Weatherley
Production: Camilla Smith

Originated by RMW
Printed and bound in China by South China Printing Company

The paper used to print this book comes from sustainable resources

ISBN 0 431 05046 5
09 08 07 06 05
10 9 8 7 6 5 4 3 2 1

British Library Cataloguing in Publication Data
Royston, Angela
How is chocolate made?
664.5

A full catalogue record for this book is available from the British Library.

Acknowledgements
The Publishers would like to thank the following for permission to reproduce photographs: Art Directors and TRIP p.**13** (Mike Shirley); BCCCA p. **9**; Corbis Sygma pp. **17**, **18**, **19** (Richard Melloul); Corbis/ Reuters/ Oswaldo Rivas p. **5**; Corbis/Royalty-Free pp. **24**, **25**; Getty Images p.**12**; Getty Images pp. **28** (PhotoDisc), **28** (Stone); Getty Images/ Issouf Sanogo p. **6**; Green and Blacks p. **8**; Harcourt Education Ltd/Tudor Photography pp. **4**, **14**, **15**, **22**, **23**, **26**, **27**, **29**; Kim Naylor p. **7**; Science Photo Library pp.**11** (Mauro Fermariello), **16** (Rosenfeld Images Ltd), **20** (Tim Hazael); Still Pictures p.**10** (Ron Giling);TopFoto p. **21**.

Cover photograph of chocolate reproduced with permission of Harcourt Education Ltd/Tudor Photography.

Disclaimer
All Internet addresses (URLs) given in this book were valid at the time of going to press. However, due to the dynamic nature of the Internet, some addresses may have changed, or sites may have changed or ceased to exist since publication. While the author and Publishers regret any inconvenience this may cause readers, no responsibility for any such changes can be accepted by either the author or the Publishers.

Every effort has been made to contact copyright holders of any material reproduced in this book. Any omissions will be rectified in subsequent printings if notice is given to the Publishers.

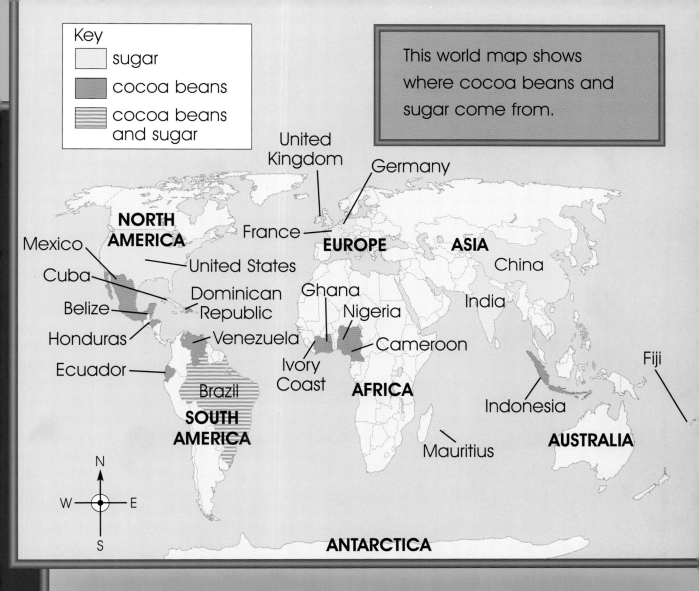

Key
- ☐ sugar
- ▨ cocoa beans
- ▤ cocoa beans and sugar

This world map shows where cocoa beans and sugar come from.

United Kingdom
Germany
France
EUROPE
ASIA
China
India

NORTH AMERICA
Mexico
Cuba
Belize
Honduras
Ecuador
United States
Dominican Republic
Venezuela
Brazil
SOUTH AMERICA

Ghana
Nigeria
Cameroon
Ivory Coast
AFRICA
Mauritius

Indonesia
AUSTRALIA
Fiji

N
W — E
S

ANTARCTICA

Chocolate is made from **cocoa beans**.

Chocolate also contains milk and sugar.

These **ingredients** come from many different parts of the world.

Who makes chocolate bars?

Several different **companies** make chocolate bars. Each company has one or more factories where the chocolate is made. Many people work for a chocolate company.

Some people work the machines in the chocolate factory. Other people pack the chocolate into boxes. Some make up names for the bars and **design** the wrappers.

This man's job is to check that the chocolate tastes good.

Cocoa beans

Cocoa beans grow in pods on cocoa trees. When the pods are **ripe**, the farmers cut them from the tree and take out the beans.

Workers spread out the beans in the sun to dry. They pack the dried beans into large bags. Then they send the beans to local companies. They send the beans to the chocolate **company**.

Sugar

Cocoa beans are very bitter. Lots of sugar is needed to make the chocolate taste sweet. Sugar is made from stalks of **sugar cane** or from **sugar beet**.

These stalks of sugar cane are cut by workers in Brazil.

Sugar cane is fed into machines. The machines squeeze out the sugary juice. The juice is then boiled until it turns into small **crystals** of sugar.

Milk

Cows make the milk that is used in chocolate. Milking machines suck the milk from the cows into pipes.

Once the milk is at the creamery, it is heated to kill any **germs**.

The milk is stored in a **refrigerator tank**. A milk tanker takes the milk to a **creamery**. A machine dries some of the milk.

Other ingredients

Many chocolate bars contain other **ingredients**. Flavourings, such as fruit and caramel, give some bars a particular taste.

peanuts

coconut

caramel

Peanuts, rice crisps, almonds, or other nuts are often mixed into the chocolate. Some chocolate bars are filled with coconut or crunchy biscuit.

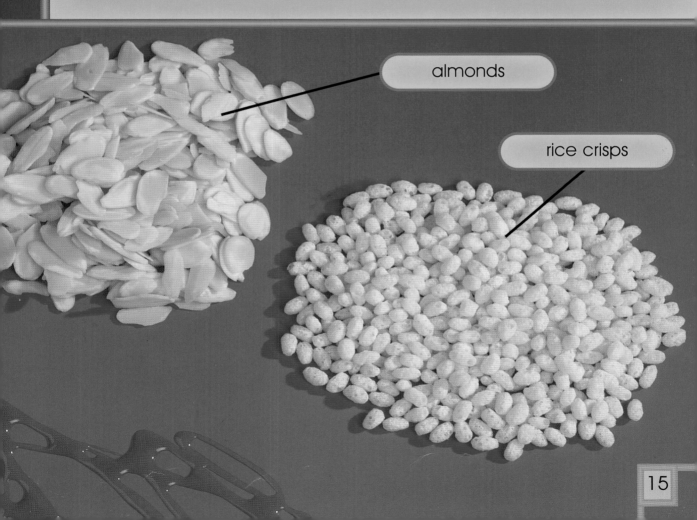

almonds

rice crisps

Preparing the cocoa beans

Ships and lorries take **cocoa beans**, sugar,
and dried milk to the chocolate factory.
Here machines clean the cocoa beans.
They take off the shells.

The beans are slowly
roasted in a machine.

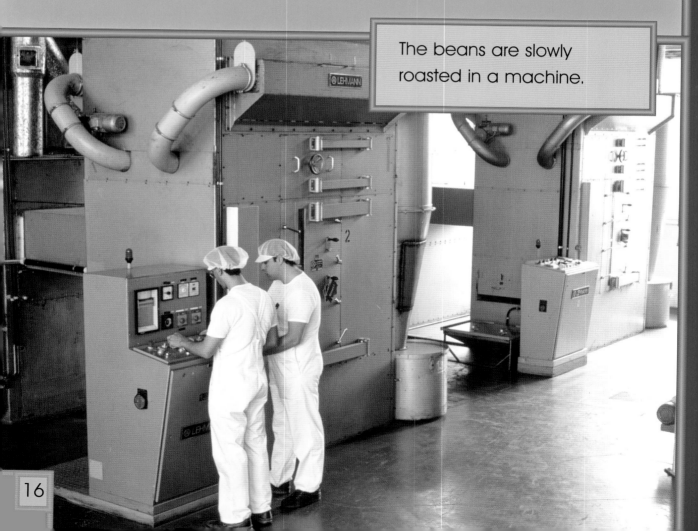

The ground beans turn into a solid called cocoa mass.

Workers feed the roasted beans into a machine called a grinder. It grinds the hot beans into small pieces. The ground beans are then cooled.

Mixing in sugar and milk

Sugar and milk powder are mixed into the cocoa mass to make a soft dough. The dough moves through rollers. They squash it into a fine powder.

The mixture is heated to change it into a liquid. The liquid is stirred for twelve hours.

The liquid now smells very chocolatey!

Bars of chocolate

While the chocolate mixture is still hot,
it pours from the trough into **moulds**.
Each mould is the shape of a single
chocolate bar.

These moulds have **ridges** to divide the chocolate into chunks.

The moulds move through a **refrigerator**. As the chocolate cools, it changes into a solid. Then the moulds are taken off. Now you can see the bars of chocolate!

Chocolate wrappers

The bars of solid milk chocolate move along a **conveyor belt**. A machine puts a wrapper around each bar.

The wrapper keeps out the air and keeps the chocolate fresh.

The bars of chocolate are then packed into boxes. Each box contains the same kind of chocolate bar.

Storing the chocolate

Lorries take the boxes of chocolate bars to a **warehouse**. The warehouse is always kept at the same cool temperature. This stops the chocolate from melting.

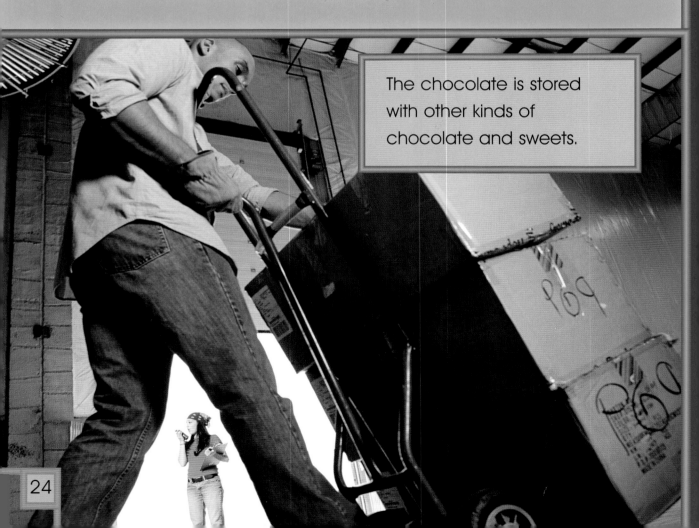

The chocolate is stored with other kinds of chocolate and sweets.

When a shop needs some more chocolate bars to sell, they order them from the warehouse. A lorry takes boxes of chocolate bars to the shop.

Selling the chocolate bars

Many kinds of shops sell chocolate bars. The shopkeeper stacks them on racks so that you can choose the kind of chocolate bar you want.

The shopkeeper pays the chocolate **company** for the bars. The chocolate company uses the money to pay its workers, and to make more chocolate bars.

Some of the money you pay for a bar of chocolate goes to the chocolate company.

From start to finish

Cocoa beans are cleaned, roasted, and ground.

Different cocoa ingredients are mixed with sugar and milk products.

The mixture is heated to make it liquid.

The liquid is poured into **moulds** and cooled to make bars of chocolate.

A closer look

A chocolate bar wrapper tells you about the **ingredients** in the chocolate bar.

STORE IN A COOL DRY PLACE

Ingredients: sugar, Fairtrade cocoa butter, dried cream whole milk powder, Fairtade cocoa mass, cocoa mass, emulsifier: soya lecithin (non GM), real vanilla.
Cocoa solids: minimum 28%.
Milk solids: minimum 20%
Fairtrade ingredients 24%

MAY CONTAIN TRACES OF NUTS AND WHEAT

Ingredients

NUTRITION INFORMATION PER

Energy	2260kj/541kcal
Protein	6.6g
Carbohydrate	57.7g
Fat	31.5g

Glossary

bitter not sweet

cocoa bean seed of the cocoa plant

company group of people who work together

conveyor belt machine that carries things on a long loop from one place to another

creamery factory that makes things from milk, such as butter, cheese, and powdered milk

crystal clear, solid piece

design decide how something will look

germ tiny living thing that can make you ill

ingredients things that are mixed together to make something

mould hollow container

refrigerator tank or large container that is kept cool

ridge narrow strip that is higher than the surface around it

ripe when seeds are ready to fall off the plant

sugar beet plant whose roots can be used to make sugar

sugar cane plant whose stem can be used to make sugar

warehouse building where things are stored

Places to visit

Cadbury World, Birmingham: museum devoted to Cadbury's chocolate, but you must book your visit in advance.

Websites:

www.bccca.org.uk
This website has information about ingredients and sustainable cocoa growing.

www.barry-callebaut.com
This website contains a history of chocolate and an explanation of how chocolate is made.

www.cadburylearingzone.co.uk
This website includes information on what life was like in a chocolate factory 100 years ago.

www.cocoatree.org
This website gives information about cocoa farming, including what life is like on a cocoa farm.

Index

Titles in the *How Are Things Made?* series include:

Hardback   0 431 05047 3

Hardback   0 431 05044 9

Hardback   0 431 05046 5

Hardback   0 431 05048 1

Hardback   0 431 05045 7

Find out about other Heinemann Library titles on our website www.heinemann.co.uk/library